Read & Respond

Ages
7–11

CW01263904

PAGE
1

Read & Respond

Ages 7–11

Author: Gillian Howell

Commissioning Editor: Rachel Mackinnon

Editor: Anna Woodford

Assistant Editor: Kim Vernon

Series Designer: Anna Oliwa

Designer: Dan Prescott

Text © 2011 Gillian Howell © 2011 Scholastic Ltd

Designed using Adobe InDesign

Published by Scholastic Ltd,
Book End, Range Road, Witney,
Oxfordshire OX29 0YD
www.scholastic.co.uk

Printed by Bell & Bain
1 2 3 4 5 6 7 8 9   1 2 3 4 5 6 7 8 9 0

British Library Cataloguing-in-Publication Data
A catalogue record for this book is available from the British Library.

ISBN 978-1407-12705-7

Acknowledgements

The publishers gratefully acknowledge permission to reproduce the following copyright material: **Random House Children's Books** for the use of extracts and the cover from *The Silver Sword* by Ian Serraillier. Text © 1956, Ian Serraillier (1956, Jonathan Cape Ltd).

Every effort has been made to trace copyright holders for the works reproduced in this book, and the publishers apologise for any inadvertent omissions.

The Silver Sword

About the book

The Silver Sword tells the story of Ruth, Edek and Bronia Balicki as they search for their parents in war-torn Europe. The story begins in Warsaw in Poland when their father, Joseph, is taken away to a prison camp. Then, when Nazi soldiers take their mother away to work in Germany, the three children escape and live on the streets of Warsaw and in the woods. Ruth starts a school for other lost children and Edek helps smuggle food to sell on the black market. But one day he disappears.

Joseph escapes from the prison camp and returns to try to find his family. All he finds in the ruins of their home is a silver paper knife (the silver sword) and a street child called Jan. Jan has survived by being an accomplished thief and pickpocket. Joseph gives the silver sword to Jan on condition that, if Jan ever meets Joseph's children, he will tell them to find him in Switzerland. Jan keeps the silver sword in his only possession – a wooden box filled with secret treasures. They become friends and Jan helps Joseph to escape from Warsaw for the journey to Switzerland in the hope of meeting his wife and children again.

Much later, Ruth and Bronia find an ill and starving boy (Jan) near the cellar where they live. One day they find the silver sword and realise Jan has met their father. Together they travel to find Edek and eventually the four of them embark on the long, dangerous journey to Switzerland to find the children's mother and father. On the journey, they encounter many dangers and difficulties but also many people who help them. Throughout their journey, the silver sword is an emblem of hope for the children. The children survive all the perils and hardship of their journey and eventually are reunited with their mother and father in Switzerland.

The story deals with the themes of love, hope, faith, separation, honesty, courage, perseverance and survival. It was televised as a mini-series in 1957.

About the author

Ian Serraillier was born in London in 1912, two years before the outbreak of the First World War. He studied classics at Oxford University and in adult life he became a school teacher, poet and author. Before writing *The Silver Sword*, he had already written 19 books for children, including retelling some myths and legends for school children. He began writing *The Silver Sword* in 1951, six years after the end of the Second World War. As he was still working as a teacher, it took him five years to complete the story during the school holidays. Ian Serraillier was a Quaker and pacifist. During the war, he was registered as a conscientious objector, so he had no first-hand experience of the conditions suffered by children like the characters, but used extensive research to describe war-torn Europe. Ian Serraillier died in 1994.

> **Facts and figures**
> **Title:** *The Silver Sword*
> **Author:** Ian Serraillier
> **Illustrator:** David Frankland, 2003
> **First published:** 1956 by Jonathan Cape
> **Television:** In 1957, and again in 1971, the BBC produced an eight-part children's series at the Lime Grove Studios in London.
> **Audio:** Puffin produced an abridged edition audio book in 2001, read by Michael Maloney.

Guided reading

Introducing the book

Together with the children, look at the cover and read the title and the name of the author. Ask the children to explore the cover illustration and describe any clues it gives about the story, such as the swastika symbol, railway lines and steam trains, and the names of foreign places. Ask them to turn to the back cover and read the blurb. Ask: *What sort of story do you expect this to be?* (Historical adventure story.)

Chapters 1 to 5

Chapters 1 to 5 introduce the background to the children's journey to find their parents by telling the story of their father Joseph's imprisonment and escape. You might find it helpful to introduce the pronunciation of certain names before the children begin reading. For example, Zakyna (*Zak*inna), Czechs (Checks), River Sanajec (Sanayec) and Mrs Krause (Krowsuh, with 'ow' as in now). Invite the children to read up to the end of Chapter 5. At the end of each chapter, pause and ask the children to summarise what they have just read: Chapter 1, Joseph escapes from the prison camp; Chapter 2, Joseph is in a cable-car and is swung down the mountain; Chapter 3, a Polish couple hide Joseph in their chalet; Chapter 4, Joseph reaches Warsaw, searches for his children and meets a boy named Jan; Chapter 5, Jan helps Joseph jump on a goods train and escape from Warsaw. At the end of Chapter 5, ask: *Which part of these chapters was the most exciting and why?* Talk about when Joseph meets Jan and ask: *What is Joseph's impression of Jan? What do you think of Jan's character? Does he really mean that he has only 'borrowed' things? Why does he keep his name secret?*

Ask the class why they think the author wrote Joseph's story at the beginning of the book?

Chapters 6 to 10

Chapters 6 to 10 describe Ruth, Bronia and Edek's life in Warsaw when they are left to fend for themselves. Edek disappears, then Ruth and Bronia find Jan, another homeless boy. They are helped by a Russian sentry named Ivan who gives them news of Edek.

Ask the children to read up to the end of Chapter 10. When they have finished, ask them to summarise the events of these chapters. Focus on Chapters 6 and 7. Ask: *Which of the children is the leader of the three and why?* Encourage them to find evidence in the text to support their ideas. (Edek takes the lead, for example, in Chapter 6: *'Come along,' said Edek. 'We shan't let them have us now.'* In Chapter 7, Edek finds a mattress and some curtains. Edek also finds casual work.)

Invite the children to describe how and why Ruth changes during the time they live in the cellar in Warsaw. (For example, she realises she must not leave everything to Edek and begins to keep Bronia cheerful. She also becomes more responsible for the other children.) Ask: *What happened to change the course of Ruth's life?* (She found Jan.)

Now focus on Chapters 9 and 10. Ask: *Why do you think Ivan helps the children?* (For example, he is impressed and intrigued by Ruth's personality.) Encourage them to observe how Jan responds to Ivan's kindness. Invite them to suggest reasons for Jan's attitude.

Chapters 11 to 18

In Chapters 11 to 18, Ruth, Bronia and Jan leave Warsaw and begin their journey on foot to Posen to find Edek who is ill with Tuberculosis (TB). Invite the children to find out about TB. What are the symptoms and why was it so difficult to treat at that time? Together, the children journey by train to Berlin where Jan befriends a chimpanzee, Bistro, that has escaped from the zoo. They continue through Germany in the Russian zone and cross into the American zone where Jan provides food for them by 'borrowing' it. Edek is worried that he is stealing from the Americans and follows Jan to find out, resulting in Edek's arrest.

Ask the children to read up to the end of

Guided reading

Chapter 18. Tell them to think about how Edek and Jan interact with each other. At the beginning of Chapter 14, explain what UNRRA workers were (the United Nations Relief and Rehabilitation Administration set up to help refugees and misplaced people after the war). When they have finished reading, ask them to summarise the events of these chapters. Ask: *How did Ruth find Edek? Was it a lucky coincidence? How do Jan and Edek feel about each other?* Invite the children to find evidence in the story to support their ideas. Ask: *How does Jan react to Jimpy's death? Did they expect him to react in this way? Why do they think Jan has such a fondness for animals?* Ask them to say why they think the author described Jan's interaction with Bistro through the viewpoint of the British officer. At the end of Chapter 17, ask: *What do you think Jan was doing to the train signal and why did Edek try to stop him? What do you think will happen to Edek now?* At the end of Chapter 18, discuss with the children why they think Jan owned up to the court. What do they think his motives were? (Pleasing and obeying Ruth rather than honesty or saving Edek.)

Chapters 19 to 23

In these chapters, Jan, Ruth, Bronia and Edek make a temporary home in a farmer's barn. The farmer lets them stay and gives them food in return for work on the farm. The local Burgomaster finds them and informs them they are to be sent back to Poland the following day. But the farmer provides two old canoes so that the children can escape during the night by river. Jan and Edek take one canoe, with Ludwig, the farm dog who has grown attached to Jan. Ruth and Bronia take the other. As they escape down river, they become separated and Ruth's canoe runs aground and is damaged. They take shelter in a haystack where Edek and Jan were on the look-out for them.

Before the children begin, read and explain the words *Bavarian* (an area of South-East Germany) and *Burgomaster* (mayor or chief official of a

German town). Invite the children to read to the end of Chapter 23. When they have finished, ask the children to summarise the events of these chapters. Ask them to say which event they think was the most dangerous for Ruth and the others. Ask them to suggest what sort of person they think the Burgomaster was. Ask: *Could he have avoided sending them back to Poland?* Then ask: *What sort of person do you think the farmer was? Why do you think he helped them escape?*

Chapters 24 to 26

In Chapter 24, Jan discovers that the silver sword is missing. He thinks they won't succeed without it, so he runs away to find it. Edek becomes more ill and collapses. But then a Polish American, Joe Wolski, gives them a lift in his lorry to a Red Cross camp near Lake Constance. There, they see Switzerland for the first time. While at the camp, the superintendent returns the silver sword to Ruth, which had been sent to the International Tracing Service (ITS), and he has also traced Ruth's father.

Invite the children to read up to the end of Chapter 25. When they have finished reading, ask: *Why do you think Jan runs off?* (He thinks the silver sword was vital to their success and wanted to get it back.) Invite the children to describe the American GI. Ask: *Why did Joe Wolski tie Jan up in the back of his lorry? Why do you think Jan burst into tears when he saw the mountains of Switzerland?* (Possible responses might be 'relief', 'release of tension at the near ending of the journey', or 'overcome with emotion' or all three.) At the beginning of Chapter 26, ask the children why Ruth is feeling disheartened. Ask: *How would you feel yourself if you were in Ruth's place?* At the end of the chapter, ask them how the children are feeling. What dangers do they think the children will now face?

Chapters 27 to 29

In these final chapters Ruth, Edek, Bronia and Jan get caught up in a severe storm. Edek gets

Guided reading

swept out onto the lake, while Ruth, Jan and Bronia try to find him. Tragedy is narrowly averted when they are rescued by a ship carrying their father, Joseph, and their mother, Margrit. Jan had behaved heroically in trying to save Ruth and Edek, during which he had lost his box of treasures. However, the silver sword was safely tied round his neck. The reunited family make their home in a new international children's village where they slowly recover from their struggles and suffering.

Before they start to read, ask the children to predict what they think might happen in the last chapters and how the story will end. Then tell the children to read to the end of Chapter 29. When they have finished, discuss their predictions and compare these with the actual story ending. Invite the children to give their opinions about the story as a whole. Ask: *Was there anything that confused or puzzled you about the story? What did you like most about the story and why? What did you dislike about the story and why? Which part of the story was the most exciting, frightening or entertaining and why?*

Shared reading

Extract 1

● Explain to the children that this extract is taken from the beginning of the story and the events take place after Edek's father, Joseph Balicki, had been taken away to a prison camp.

● Highlight the words and phrases that begin with capitals (*Warsaw, Nazi, Boys' Rifle Brigade*) and ask the children to explain why they begin with upper case letters. (Proper nouns or names.) It might be helpful to identify and explain about any historical references, such as the siege of Warsaw, Nazis, storm troopers and the Boys' Rifle Brigade.

● Encourage the children to read the text aloud together. Ask the children to describe the mood or atmosphere of the extract.

● Invite them to suggest how the author achieves the atmosphere. Ask them to underline words that describe the mood or atmosphere (*banged, catch, Quietly*). Ask them to identify different sentence types (long sentences and short sharp ones) and highlight them in the text. For example: *The door was locked. He shouted and banged on it with his fists, but it was no use.* Why do they think the author uses a variety of sentences?

● At the end of the extract ask: *If you were in Edek's place, what would you have done?*

Extract 2

● Invite the children to read the extract aloud with you.

● Ask them to underline words and phrases used to describe speech: *shouted, piped up, shrilled*. Invite the children to say how these speech verbs help them to read the spoken words.

● Ask the children to find examples of imagery and descriptive phrases that help them picture the scene. Tell them to underline or circle these phrases in the text. For example: *scurrying of rats, creaking of rusty hinges, half-darkness, vague blur of hay, over-ripe, bristling with bits of hay, The hay at the farmer's feet parted.*

● Invite the children to give reasons for the farmer's reaction to hearing something unusual in his barn. Was he afraid, concerned or simply curious? Why do they think his threat *to fetch the prong* had no effect on the children?

● Ask them to describe how hiding in the hay affected Edek. Explain what *chaff* is. (Fine bits of hay.) Ask them what the author meant when Bronia saw *the murderous prong*.

Extract 3

● Read the extract together. Ask the children to summarise the extract. Point out that this passage contains no dialogue. Invite them to suggest why that is. Possible responses might include the noise of the water, speed of movement, tiredness.

● Invite the children to think of what Ruth might say during this event if she were giving a commentary. Provide them with paper speech bubbles to add empty speech bubbles around the text. Re-read the text together, pausing at several points and ask the children to suggest what Ruth says. For example: when the spray stung their faces; when Ruth felt *a triumphant sense of exhilaration*; when *a boulder loomed up*; when *The terrors of the rapids were over*.

● Invite the children to say how the tone of the extract changes at the end of the passage. For example, the calmer atmosphere means that one reads more slowly. Ask them to underline words and phrases that indicate this calmer atmosphere: *broadened, eased, no need for the paddle now, clear of rocks, smooth, lie back.*

Shared reading

Extract 1

From Chapter 6, 'The Night of the Storm Troopers'

That night there was an inch of snow on the roofs of Warsaw. Ruth and Bronia were asleep in the bedroom next to their mother's. Edek's room was on the top floor, below the attic. He was asleep when the Nazi soldiers broke into the house, but he woke up when he heard a noise outside his door. He jumped out of bed and turned the handle. The door was locked. He shouted and banged on it with his fists, but it was no use. Then he lay down with his ear to the floor and listened. In his mother's room the men were rapping out orders, but he could not catch a word that was said.

In the ceiling was a small trapdoor that led into the attic. A ladder lay between his bed and the wall. Quietly he removed it, hooked it under the trap, and climbed up.

Hidden between the water tank and the felt jacket round it was his rifle. He was a member of the Boys' Rifle Brigade and had used it in the siege of Warsaw. It was loaded. He took it out and quickly climbed down to his room.

The noise in the room below had stopped. Looking out of the window into the street, he saw a Nazi van waiting outside the front door. Two storm troopers were taking his mother down the steps, and she was struggling.

Quietly Edek lifted the window sash till it was half open. He dared not shoot in case he hit his mother. He had to wait till she was in the van and the doors were being closed.

His first shot hit a soldier in the arm. Yelling, he jumped in beside the driver. With the next two shots Edek aimed at the tyres. One punctured the rear wheel, but the van got away, skidding and roaring up the street. His other shots went wide.

READ & RESPOND: Activities based on *The Silver Sword*

Extract 2

From Chapter 19, 'The Bavarian Farmer'

There were queer noises in the barn, louder than the scurrying of rats or the creaking of rusty hinges in the wind.

The farmer flung the door open and shouted, 'Come out of there, you young devil! I heard you – can't you imitate a rat better than that?'

He stood still, accustoming his eyes to the half-darkness of the barn. The sun rose early enough in July, but it was not full daylight yet and all he could see was a vague blur of hay. While he listened, everything was so quiet that he began to wonder if he had been mistaken.

Then the sound of a half-sob, stifled immediately, confirmed his suspicions.

'Come out!' he shouted. 'Do I smoke you out like rabbits – or fetch the prong?'

The threats were ineffective, so he went off to fetch the prong. Soon the hay was flying. And something else came flying too – an over-ripe turnip which, beautifully aimed, struck the farmer full in the nape of the neck. He swore.

An anxious voice piped up, 'We give in – please put that horrible thing away before it goes right through Bronia.' And the farmer turned round, his prong poised in mid-air, to find himself face to face with a tall thin girl, her clothes and hair bristling with bits of hay. 'We only spent the night here. We haven't done any harm.'

When she realized that he had not properly understood, Ruth called Edek.

The hay at the farmer's feet parted, and Edek's spluttering face appeared. He had held his breath all too long and made a dive for the open air, clinging to the handle of the barn door while he coughed the chaff out of his lungs.

'Hey, that's me you're stepping on!' shrilled Bronia, as she emerged from under the farmer's left foot. And when she saw the murderous prong, she flew to Ruth and hid behind her.

Shared reading

Extract 3

From Chapter 23, 'Dangerous Waters'

The river grew faster, and the bank flashed past. Soon they were in a kind of gorge, where the river squeezed past great boulders, some of them as high as houses. Some of the swells were over a foot high, and the spray dashed over the bow and stung their faces. The water roared here so that even the loudest shout could not be heard. Out to the left there were oily surges that looked as if they would pound you down into the depths if you got caught in them.

Bronia closed her eyes and clung to her sister's waist. Ruth was not as scared as she had expected to be. With a triumphant sense of exhilaration she flashed in with her paddle, heading always for the open stream, away from the white broken water where the rocks lay hidden. Now and then a boulder loomed up, and she knew that if they struck it they would be dashed to pieces. But a quick dip of the paddle at the right moment was enough to shoot them safely past.

In no time the river broadened, the boulders eased, and the banks were wooded again. The terrors of the rapids were over. Ruth hoped that Edek and Jan, whose two-seater was much less easy to manoeuvre, had been as successful as they had.

There seemed no need for the paddle now, for the water was clear of rocks and the current smooth and swift. They could lie back and let the canoe take care of itself.

Bronia closed her eyes and fell asleep. Ruth lay back and watched the blue sky overhead and the climbing sun. It was to be another scorching day, and she too became sleepy and dozed.

Text © 1956, Ian Serraillier.

READ & RESPOND: Activities based on The Silver Sword

Plot, character and setting

Warsaw

> **Objective:** To use visualisation techniques in order to empathise with characters in the setting.
> **What you need:** Copies of *The Silver Sword,* writing materials.
> **Cross-curricular link:** History.

What to do

● This activity should be run when the children have read Chapter 4.

● Invite the children to say where this chapter is set. Ask them to describe the setting orally. Encourage them to add as much detail as they can remember, for example: *crumbling walls, mountains of bricks, Windows were charred and glassless, the only really lively place was the railway.*

● Turn to the first page of Chapter 4 and point out the sentence: *The place was as bleak and silent as the craters of the moon.* Ask the children to describe what impression of Warsaw this image conveys to them (desolate, depressing, eerie, like a graveyard).

● Tell them to close their eyes and imagine they are in the setting of Warsaw. Ask them to describe the setting to a partner. Encourage them to use their senses: what can they see, hear, feel and smell?

● Provide the children with paper and pens and ask them to imagine that they are walking through a bombed city. Invite them to use the first person and write four sentences about what they can see, hear, feel and smell.

> **Differentiation**
> **For older/more confident learners:** Ask the children to write a paragraph they could use as a setting description for a story.
> **For younger/less confident learners:** Let the children focus on just two of the senses.

The railway

> **Objective:** To explore how the author uses dramatic and comic language for effect.
> **What you need:** Copies of *The Silver Sword,* writing materials.
> **Cross-curricular link:** History.

What to do

● This activity should be run when the children have read Chapter 5.

● Invite the children to work with a partner and go through the chapter to find dramatic language that describes the setting of the railway. For example, *drizzle,* an empty warehouse, broken glass, train clattered by, hiss of steam.

● Ask the children to picture themselves by the railway at night. Tell them to close their eyes and keep quiet, just like Joseph had to, so that he wouldn't be discovered by the Nazis. Ask questions to stimulate their imaginations: *When a train speeds past, what can you hear? What can you feel? What other sounds might you hear in the darkness? What smells might there be by the railway?*

● Joseph says, *Let's have something to eat'.* Ask the children what is funny (comic) about this dialogue and the rest of the paragraph that follows. *Does the author mean it to be comic? What effect does that have on the children's feelings about Joseph and Jan?* (They should feel friendlier towards them.)

● Provide the children with paper and pens and ask them to imagine that they are hiding beside a railway. Invite them to use the first person and write four sentences about what they can see, hear, feel and smell.

> **Differentiation**
> **For older/more confident learners:** Ask the children to write a paragraph they could use as a setting description for a story.
> **For younger/less confident learners:** Let the children focus on just two of the senses.

Plot, character and setting

Jan

Objective: To explore how the author uses dramatic and comic language for effective characterisation.
What you need: Copies of *The Silver Sword*, writing materials.
Cross-curricular link: History.

What to do
● Run this activity after the children have read Chapters 4 and 5.
● Invite the children to describe their first impressions of Jan. Ask them how his appearance is described when Joseph first encounters him – *small, wispy fair hair, unnaturally bright eyes.*
● Ask them to say what aspects of Jan's character intrigue Joseph and to support their ideas with evidence from the text. (His pickpocket skills, his desire for the silver sword, he listens intently to Joseph, he tells Joseph nothing about himself except his name, his survival skills.)
● Ask the children to say what intrigues them or puzzles them about Jan. Ask: *Why does he think it isn't safe to tell anyone his name?*
● Remind the children that Jan steals from Joseph and also helps him escape from Warsaw. Ask: *Do you think the author wants you to think Jan is a good character or a bad character? What makes you think that?*
● Provide the children with a blank sheet of paper. Ask them to draw a stick figure to represent Jan and ask them to add words and phrases for a character sketch of Jan.

Differentiation
For older/more confident learners: Ask them to imagine Jan's background and add words and phrases to give a fuller picture of Jan's character.
For younger/less confident learners: Ask the children to work in small groups and collaborate to describe Jan.

The Russian sentry

Objective: To take account of different viewpoints, explaining how characters might see events from different points of view.
What you need: Copies of *The Silver Sword*.
Cross-curricular link: History.

What to do
● Do this activity after the children have read Chapters 9 and 10.
● Ask the children to say whether the story is told in the first person or third person voice. *Is the story told from any one person's point of view?* (It is told from the author's point of view.)
● Ask the children to suggest how these chapters might be written differently if told from Jan's point of view. For example, in first person, some events might be told through dialogue or reportage where the narrator was not present.
● Ask the children to work with a partner on the events involving Ivan, the Russian sentry. Explain that you want them to go through the text together and, using the first person voice from Ivan's point of view, work out how to describe the events. Give them an example to stimulate their ideas. (You could use the time when Ruth came to see Ivan: 'I was on sentry duty when a young girl came and stood staring at me.')
● Invite some pairs to share their ideas in a plenary session. Ask them to describe how the impact of the story changes when told only from one person's point of view. Do they think it adds anything to the reader's enjoyment or detracts from it? Ask them to give reasons for their opinions.

Differentiation
For older/more confident learners: Ask them to repeat the activity using Ruth as a first person narrator and say how the two versions compare.
For younger/less confident learners: Ask the children to use a first-person Ruth as narrator and describe how she went to ask Ivan for shoes.

Plot, character and setting

Impressions of Ruth

Objective: To explore a character from other characters' points of view.
What you need: Copies of *The Silver Sword*, photocopiable page 15.
Cross-curricular link: History.

What to do
● Complete this activity after reading the whole book.
● Discuss with the class their ideas about Ruth's character and personality. Questions you could ask to stimulate their responses include: *Ruth looks after Bronia and Jan – does she ever moan or complain about this? What acts of kindness or generosity does Ruth perform for others? How does Ruth respond to figures of authority? How does Ruth react to danger?* Ask them to support their ideas with reference to the text.
● Invite the children to skim-read through the text and find examples of how the following characters in the story respond to Ruth, and what

their impressions of her are. Other characters include: the lieutenant in Chapter 9; Ivan, the Russian sentry in Chapters 9 and 10; and Mark, the British officer, in Chapter 15.
● Provide the children with photocopiable page 15 and ask them to write down words and phrases used in the text to describe Ruth from the viewpoint of the characters.
● Collate the children's findings and compare the impressions these characters have of Ruth with the children's own impressions as discussed at the beginning of the activity.

Differentiation
For older/more confident learners: Ask them to add another character from the story, for example Herr Wolff or the Burgomaster.
For younger/less confident learners: Ask the children to write notes of key words or phrases about Ruth from one character's viewpoint, sharing the three characters among the group.

What happened when…?

Objective: To recall and sequence the events of the story, to explain and understand cause and effect.
What you need: Copies of *The Silver Sword*, photocopiable page 16.
Cross-curricular link: History.

What to do
● This activity should be run when the children have read the whole book.
● Before the children do the activity independently in their groups, ask them a few cause-and-effect questions from the beginning of the story, such as: *What happened when Joseph Balicki turned a picture of Hitler to the wall?* Ask them to scan the text to find the answer.
● Provide the groups with sets of the cards on photocopiable page 16 and give a set to each group, face downwards.
● Invite one child to pick a card and read the

card to another child, beginning with the words, *What happened when… ?* The other child describes what happened immediately after as a result of the event on the card.
● Continue round the group until all the cards have been used and everyone has had a turn at asking and answering.
● Finally, ask the group to collaborate to put the cards into the sequence of events in the story.

Differentiation
For older/more confident learners: Ask the children to put two events next to each other that were not sequential in the story and to explore/make up what might link those two events.
For younger/less confident learners: Let the children refer to the story to find the answers to the questions.

Plot, character and setting

Journeys

> **Objective:** To understand the effect of key events on the plot by making notes across the text to explain them.
> **What you need:** Copies of *The Silver Sword*, photocopiable page 17.
> **Cross-curricular links:** History, geography.

What to do

● This activity should be run when the children have read the whole book.

● Ask the children to turn to the map at the end of the story. Explain what the map illustrates. Invite the children to describe any events they recall that happened along the route of the journey.

● Ask them to say why they recall these events. Ask: *What is significant about the effect of these events on the story?*

● Hand out photocopiable page 17. Ask the children to refer to the text and to annotate their maps with what they think are the six key events of the story.

● Ask some children to show their story-maps to the class and compare their annotations. Invite them to explain why they chose certain events as key events. Compare any differences in their choices and invite them to discuss which should be included and which omitted.

> **Differentiation**
> **For older/more confident learners:** Ask the children to expand to eight key events and to explain, in one sentence, why each is significant.
> **For younger/less confident learners:** Let the children work as a group to collaborate on their choices of key events.

That charming bundle of good intentions and atrocious deeds

> **Objective:** To explore how and why an author creates a character and the character's impact on the plot.
> **What you need:** Copies of *The Silver Sword*, photocopiable page 18.
> **Cross-curricular link:** History.

What to do

● This activity should be run when the children have read the whole book.

● Ask the children to talk with a partner for a few minutes about the character of Jan. What do they know about him? Invite some of them to share their impressions about Jan with the others.

● Ask the children to explain how important a character Jan is to the plot. Ask: *Why do you think the author included Jan in the story? How would the story be different if Jan did not feature?*

● At the end of the book, the author calls Jan: *that charming bundle of good intentions and atrocious deeds.* What do they think this means? Ask: *Can you think of any good intentions or atrocious deeds committed by Jan?*

● Hand out photocopiable page 18. Invite the children to skim-read through the text and add details of Jan's actions to the page, while deciding if they are good intentions or atrocious deeds.

● When they have finished, share and compare the children's decisions about Jan. If there are any of Jan's actions that they have put into both categories, ask them to explain why.

> **Differentiation**
> **For older/more confident learners:** Ask them to write a paragraph to say why they think Jan is either basically good or basically bad.
> **For younger/less confident learners:** Let the children work in a group with an adult and discuss Jan's actions to reach a group decision about his character.

SECTION
4

Impressions of Ruth

● Find words and phrases from the story that show how the lieutenant, Ivan (the Russian sentry) and Mark (the British officer) feel and think about Ruth. Write them in the blank spaces.

The lieutenant	
Ivan, the Russian sentry	
Mark, the British officer	

Plot, character and setting

What happened when…?

● Cut out the cards and ask 'What happened when…?'

The storm troopers took Margrit Balicki away.	Edek secretly followed Jan when he left hay-making early.	Ruth and Bronia's canoe got stuck under the bridge.
The superintendant of the Red Cross camp called Ruth to his office.	Jan was given a bowl of soup at the field kitchen in the village of Kolina.	They spent the night in the Bavarian farmer's barn.
Jan discovered the silver sword was missing from his box.	Joe Wolski gave them a lift in his lorry.	They went down to the lakeside to see the Swiss boat that would take them over the water.

READ & RESPOND: Activities based on *The Silver Sword*

Plot, character and setting

Journeys

- Mark the location of six key events on the map to make a story-map.
- Annotate the locations with a title of each of the six events you choose. For example: Spending the night in the Bavarian farmer's barn.

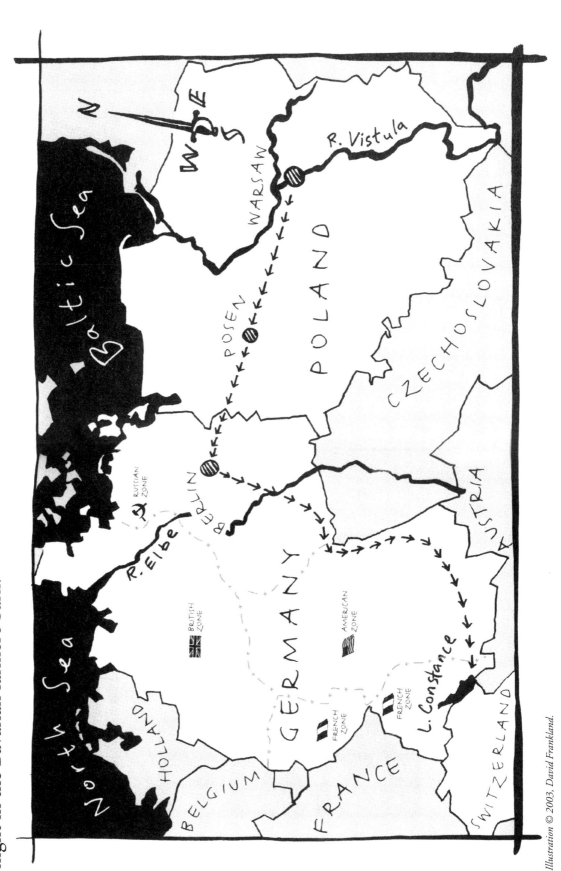

Illustration © 2003, David Frankland.

That charming bundle of good intentions and atrocious deeds

● In Chapter 29, the author describes Jan as *that charming bundle of good intentions and atrocious deeds*. Look through the text and choose the things that you think Jan did with good intentions. Then look through again and choose things that Jan did that you think were atrocious deeds. Add them to the columns below.

● Here are three suggestions to help you:
  ● Stealing food from the Nazis
  ● Helping Joseph jump a train
  ● Giving Bistro the chimpanzee a cigarette

Good intentions	Atrocious deeds

Talk about it

Finding out about Jan

Objective: To use and explore a variety of questions to understand a character better.
What you need: Copies of *The Silver Sword*, photocopiable page 22.
Cross-curricular link: History.

What to do
● This activity should be done when the children have read the whole book.
● Talk about what a complex character Jan is with the children for a few minutes. Do they like or dislike Jan and why? Ask: *Is there anything that puzzles you about Jan? Are there any questions about him that weren't answered in the story?*
● Encourage them to suggest what they would like to ask Jan if they met him. Invite volunteers to take turns to sit in the hot seat in the role of Jan.
● Cut out the question starter cards on photocopiable page 22 and share them among the other children.
● Invite them to ask Jan a question beginning with one of the question starters. Encourage 'Jan' to answer based on their knowledge of him from the story but also to use their imagination to add their own ideas about Jan, his motives and background.
● When they have finished, invite them to say whether, and how, the hot seat activity helped them to understand Jan better.

Differentiation
For older/more confident learners: Ask them to generate their own questions to pose to Jan.
For younger/less confident learners: Let the children read the question cards and work out suitable questions together before running the activity.

Freeze-frame

Objective: To use drama strategies and conventions to explore themes in the text.
What you need: Copies of *The Silver Sword*, writing materials.
Cross-curricular link: History.

What to do
● This activity can be run at any point in the story.
● Explain that the children are going to 'pause the story', as if they were pausing a film, and create a freeze-frame moment.
● Choose a moment from the story that reflects one of its themes in order to demonstrate how this is done. (For example: when Edek is caught smuggling and is taken away – separation; when the farmer discovers them hiding in his barn – courage or survival.) Discuss what each character might be thinking and hoping at this moment.
● Organise the children into small groups of different numbers of children so they will be able to choose different scenes from across the book.
● Ask the children to look through the book and choose a scene from the story that suits the number of children in their group. Ask them to allocate characters to each child in the group and, using a sheet of paper and a pen, collaborate to work out how the scene might look.
● Invite each group to show their chosen scene as a freeze-frame, group by group. Encourage each child in the scene to describe what they are thinking and hoping for at that moment and say what they will do next.

Differentiation
For older/more confident learners: Ask them to write a description of their group's scene.
For younger/less confident learners: Encourage the children to draw a picture of their group's freeze-frame moment.

Talk about it

Conscience alley

> **Objective:** To use drama techniques to explore a dilemma in the text.
> **What you need:** Copies of *The Silver Sword*, photocopiable page 23, scissors.
> **Cross-curricular link:** History.

What to do

● This activity can be run at any point in the story.

● Choose a dilemma or decision from the story. (For example: when Jan decides to return to find the silver sword after it goes missing, or when Edek gets put on trial for interfering with the train signal.)

● Invite a volunteer to take on the role, for example, of Jan. Explain that the other children should consider what advice they would give Jan to influence his decision.

● Arrange the children in two lines facing each other. You may want to ask one line to take one stance, for example, advice on why he should go to find the sword (it's good luck). The other line should give the opposite advice on why to leave the sword (it's too dangerous to go back).

● Encourage the children to give reasons for their advice, such as: 'Ruth and Bronia might be in more danger without you.'

● Invite 'Jan' to walk down 'conscience alley' while the children take turns to whisper their advice to him.

● Ask the volunteer to then say what his decision will be.

● Hand out photocopiable page 23 and ask the children to cut out and order the statements in order of importance.

> **Differentiation**
> **For older/more confident learners:** Ask the children to write a paragraph explaining potential consequences of Jan's decision.
> **For younger/less confident learners:** Let the children work with a partner to discuss and order the statements. Ask them to choose the one they think is the most important.

Soundscape

> **Objective:** To use drama techniques to create impact.
> **What you need:** Copies of *The Silver Sword*, writing materials.

What to do

● This activity can be run at any point in the story.

● Choose a setting from any part of the story, such as at the railway in Warsaw or during the storm at Lake Constance.

● Arrange the children into small groups and ask them to discuss what they would be able to hear in this setting. You might like to let them close their eyes to help them imagine this.

● Ask each group to allocate the sounds for their setting to each member. Encourage them to try out different ways of making their sounds using their voices, hands or feet. Invite them to sit on the floor in their group and recreate the sounds experienced in the setting.

● Extend the activity by asking the groups to choose another setting from the story, work out a soundscape for it and perform it for the other children. Ask the other children to guess what part of the story is being recreated and say how the soundscape made them feel.

> **Differentiation**
> **For older/more confident learners:** Ask the children to write a paragraph describing what can be heard in the setting.
> **For younger/less confident learners:** Invite the children to draw the setting and label the sounds.

Talk about it

What happened in between?

> **Objective:** To role play a scene between chapters, identifying dramatic ways of conveying characters' ideas and building tension.
> **What you need:** Copies of *The Silver Sword*, writing materials.

What to do
● This activity should be run when the children have read Chapters 12 and 13.
● Remind the children that in Chapter 12, Ruth finds Edek, and the next chapter begins when the family are travelling on a train. If needed, ask them to remind themselves by re-reading the text.
● Allow the children time to work out a new scene that takes them from the field kitchen in Chapter 12 to the train to Berlin.
● Arrange the children into groups of four or five. Ask them to discuss what they think might have happened between these two points in the story. Encourage them to experiment with dialogue. For example, who would explain to Edek about Jan? Ask: *What might Jan and Edek say to each other?* Do they need another character, for example, another adult or authority figure? Ask: *How did they get onto the train?*
● Invite each group to perform their new scene for the others.

> **Differentiation**
> **For older/more confident learners:** Ask the children to make notes of ideas for their new scene to be used for writing. (Provide them with an example of a drama dialogue to use for structure.)
> **For younger/less confident learners:** Work with the children in a group to stimulate their ideas for the new scene. Scribe their ideas and let them use these during the role play.

Endings or beginnings?

> **Objective:** To discuss how underlying themes and points of view affect the emotions of the characters.
> **What you need:** Copies of *The Silver Sword*, photocopiable page 24.

What to do
● This activity should be run when the children have read Chapter 28.
● Remind the children that in Chapter 28, Ruth, Edek and Bronia are reunited with their parents after not seeing them for at least four years and that Jan meets them for the first time.
● Draw up a list of words to describe how they might feel. (Relief, happiness, nervousness, awkwardness, excitement, and so on.)
● Discuss how the emotions of each character might differ. For example, how would Margrit Balicki's feelings be different from Jan's or Bronia's?
● Arrange the children into groups and ask them to think about what each character might hope for the future. For example, might the children want to return to Poland or Jan to become part of the family? Encourage them to discuss this for a few minutes.
● Cut out the character cards from the photocopiable page 24 and place them face down for each group. Invite one child at a time to pick out a card, read the name and then describe how they felt when they were all reunited and what they were hoping would happen in the future.
● Invite the groups to comment on how similar or different each group's responses were.

> **Differentiation**
> **For older/more confident learners:** Ask the children to choose their favourite character and describe how they feel and their future hopes in more detail.
> **For younger/less confident learners:** Invite the children to suggest how they would feel in the same situation.

Talk about it

Finding out about Jan

- Cut out the question starters below.
- Get into pairs and take it in turns to ask the questions and 'be' Jan.
- 'Jan' must answer based on your knowledge of him from the story but you can also use your imagination to add your own ideas about Jan, his motives and background.
- When you have finished, talk about whether, and how, the hot seat activity helped you to understand Jan better.

What was your first impression of…?	Why did you…?
Why didn't you…?	When were you most…?
What didn't you like about…?	Who would you like to…?
How did you feel about…?	What did you think when Ruth…?
How did you feel when Jimpy…?	What did you think when…?
What would you do differently…?	What would you change about…?

READ & RESPOND: Activities based on The Silver Sword

Conscience alley

● Cut out the statements and put them in the order you think is most important.

If Jan returns to find the silver sword...

✂

he won't be able to find the family again.
Ruth, Bronia and Edek will be lonely.
Ruth, Bronia and Edek will run out of food.
he might be caught and sent back to Poland.
he might get into danger.
their luck will come back again.
the family will be grateful to him.
it will mean they will succeed in finding their parents in Switzerland.

Talk about it

Endings or beginnings?

- Cut out the character cards.
- Place them face down.
- Taking it in turns, pick out a card, read the name and then:
  - describe how the character felt when they were all reunited.
  - describe what they were hoping would happen in the future.

Bronia	Edek
Ruth	Jan
Joseph	Margrit

Get writing

Dear Mum

Objective: To select words and language, drawing on knowledge of literary features and formal and informal writing.
What you need: Copies of *The Silver Sword*, writing materials.

What to do
● Run this activity when the children have read to the end of Chapter 7. The children will write a letter from Ruth to her mother after discussing the characters.
● Discuss what has happened in the story so far, focusing on Bronia. Invite them to share what they think Bronia must be feeling and thinking without her mother. Remind them that Bronia was only three when her mother was taken.
● Now focus on Ruth. Ask the children to describe the role that Ruth was forced to take in the family without their parents. Ask: *How might Ruth have felt about this?*

● Ask the children to suggest, if they were Ruth, what they would say to their mother about what was happening. Ask them some questions to stimulate their ideas such as: *Do you think Ruth would complain? Would she want to reassure her mother that they were alright? How might she do this? What would she say about Edek? Would she ask any questions?* Add their responses to the board.
● Remind the children about the layout of a letter and ask them to write a letter from Ruth to her mother.

For older/more confident learners: Encourage the children to write their letters in six paragraphs covering reassurance, circumstances, Jan, Ruth's worries, some questions for her mother, conclusion.
For younger/less confident learners: Work with the children in a group and provide them with a letter framework of sentence starters and limit it to three paragraphs.

The fight for Warsaw

Objective: To understand the sequence of events using connectives, and varied structures, to shape and organise the text coherently.
What you need: Copies of *The Silver Sword*, photocopiable pages 28 and 29, scissors.
Cross-curricular link: History.

What to do
● Run this activity when the children have read the beginning of Chapter 8, up to the point when Warsaw falls into Russian hands.
● Invite the children to recall what happened in their own words. Write their responses as bullet-point notes on the board. Discuss the sequence of the events as recalled by the children. Do they remember them in the correct sequence? Ask them to suggest linking words that show the sequence, such as 'first', 'next', 'at the same moment', 'simultaneously', 'later', and so on.

● Talk with the children about the importance of accuracy when writing a historical account of events.
● Provide the children with photocopiable page 28. Ask them to cut out the events and re-order them in the correct sequence.
● Provide them with photocopiable page 29. Ask them to cut out the connectives and choose the most appropriate ones to add to the events.
● Invite some of the children to share their results with the others.

Differentiation
For older/more confident learners: Encourage the children to rewrite the events in their own words, using connectives to show the sequence.
For younger/less confident learners: Let the children refer to the text to work out the sequence.

Get writing

Support the international children's village!

> **Objective:** To use persuasive language to sway the reader.
> **What you need:** Copies of *The Silver Sword.*

What to do

- Run this activity when the children have read Chapter 29 'The New Beginning.'
- Invite the children to read the beginning of the chapter to: *When they grew up, they would be able to meet the future with goodwill and courage.*
- Ask: *What was the purpose of the international children's village and how was the project funded?* Write up their points on the board.
- Explain that they are going to persuade people around the world to support the village. Ask them to suggest what sort of support would help the project. Ask: *What could people do to help?*

- Ask them to talk, in pairs, about how to raise awareness of the international children's village. Draw up a list of their suggestions.
- Choose one suggestion and use shared writing to note ideas of persuasive devices to attract attention and influence people. Ask the children to think of persuasive words and phrases, such as alliterative slogans and emotive vocabulary.
- Ask the children to choose a persuasive format and create their own poster or advertisement.

> **Differentiation**
> **For older/more confident learners:** Encourage the children to use a computer to create a campaign to support the project using presentation software.
> **For younger/less confident learners:** Ask the children to create a persuasive poster.

Lost for over a year!

> **Objective:** To write about a character's experiences to extend achievement and experience in writing.
> **What you need:** Copies of *The Silver Sword.*

What to do

- Run this activity when the children have read to the end of Chapter 13 and after they have worked on the activity, 'What happened in between?'
- Invite the children to recount how Edek became lost and what happened to him.
- Point out the section in Chapter 13 where Edek describes hiding in a train. Ask the children to use their own words to describe what happened to Edek during the year he was missing, using the third person voice.
- Explain that they are to split into three groups: one to write about how Edek became lost; the second to write Edek's story about his experiences of slaving on the land in Germany; and the third to write about escaping on the train.

- Use shared writing to draft opening lines for each section, such as: 'During Edek's last smuggling trip, the secret police were waiting for him.'
- Invite the children to suggest how to add detail about what Edek saw, heard and felt. Repeat for the other two sections.
- Tell the children to think about how to end each section so that it flows into the next. For example, 'When things began to go badly for the Nazis, Edek took his chance to escape.'
- Divide the children into three groups and allocate a section of Edek's story to each one.

> **Differentiation**
> **For older/more confident learners:** Ask pairs to work together, each writing one section but collaborating to ensure it flows as a complete recount.
> **For younger/less confident learners:** Let them write a group story for one section of Edek's story.

Get writing

Play time

> **Objective:** To extend achievement and experience in writing by creating a new episode as a playscript.
> **What you need:** Copies of *The Silver Sword*.

What to do

- Run this activity when the children have read to the end of Chapter 13 and after the children have worked on the activity 'What happened in between?'
- Invite the children to say how they feel when they have found something that they thought was lost. Ask: *How must Ruth and Bronia have felt when they found Edek?*
- Explain that they are going to write a short scene for a play to show when the girls and Jan meet up with Edek again in the field camp.
- Remind the children about the conventions of playscript writing, such as having a cast list and including some text to set the scene of the action. They should put the cast names on the left of the page, include any stage directions (character movements), and there should be no use of speech verbs or speech punctuation.
- Invite the children to suggest what the characters would say to each other and what actions they might take. Ask: *How might Jan's responses and behaviour differ from those of Ruth and Bronia?* Use shared writing to demonstrate how to lay out the playscript by scribing some of the children's suggestions.
- Invite the children to write a short scene showing the meeting.
- Share some of the children's scripts and invite groups of four to act out some of the scripts.

> **Differentiation**
> **For older/more confident learners:** Encourage them to write their playscript as a cartoon strip using speech bubbles.
> **For younger/less confident learners:** Let the children work in small groups of four and role play the meeting before writing. An adult could scribe for them during the role play.

Ruth Balicki ~ house mother

> **Objective:** To use description about a character and write in a different style to extend experience in writing.
> **What you need:** Copies of *The Silver Sword*, photocopiable page 30.

What to do

- Run this activity when the children have read the whole book.
- Invite the children to describe Ruth's life using their own words.
- Discuss what became of Ruth when she became an adult.
- Explain that they are going to write a biography of Ruth's life.
- Revise the features of biographies with the children, such as chronological order, past tense, third person verbs, dates and personal details of the subject.
- Brainstorm a list of information about Ruth that would be useful to include in a biography.
- Provide the children with photocopiable page 30 and ask them to work in groups, using the text to find out details about Ruth and add them to the page.
- Invite the children to use the notes they made on the photocopiable sheet to write a biography of Ruth.

> **Differentiation**
> **For older/more confident learners:** Encourage the children to write notes about details and dates without using the photocopiable sheet.
> **For younger/less confident learners:** Let the children work with a partner and take turns to find information while the other partner adds notes to the photocopiable sheet.

Get writing

The fight for Warsaw 1

● Cut out the rows and re-order them in the correct sequence.

Warsaw was in Russian hands.
Radio Moscow appealed to the Poles in Warsaw for support.
The Russian Marshal Rokossovsky was sweeping westward towards Warsaw with seven army troops.
The Poles, under General Bor, rose up against the German garrison in Warsaw.
The Russian (Soviet) troops withdrew by six miles, leaving the Poles on their own.
Stalin changed his mind.
The Nazis left Warsaw.
The Poles were short of ammunition and appealed to the British and Americans.
The Germans counter-attacked and their tanks drove a wedge through the city.
The British and Americans were too busy fighting to help, but they asked Stalin, the Russian leader, to help the Poles.
Warsaw broadcast a last appeal to the world for help.
Stalin refused to help.

The fight for Warsaw 2

● Cut out the connecting words and phrases and use them to show the sequence of the recount of events.

In the summer of 1944	At the same time	Simultaneously
By January 1945	At once	Then
Immediately	Later	Now
However	Unfortunately	Finally
At last	Eventually	But

Get writing

Ruth Balicki – house mother

- Look through the story to find details about Ruth's life.
- Add the details you find to the chart below.
- Use your notes to write a biography of Ruth.

When was she born?	
Where was she born?	
What sort of place was she born in?	
Who were her brothers and sisters?	
What profession did her parents have?	
What significant events occurred while she was growing up?	
What happened to Ruth when she became an adult?	
What important dates should you include?	
Any other information?	

Assessment

Assessment advice

The Silver Sword is a moving story about a family torn apart by war. With its themes of love, hope, faith, separation, honesty, courage, perseverance and survival, it appeals to children on many levels. It begins by describing Joseph Balicki's determination to escape from a prison camp to find his family, but the majority of the book tells about the children's struggles to survive in Warsaw under the Nazis and their subsequent journey from Warsaw to Switzerland to be eventually reunited with their parents.

During this period they suffer extraordinary deprivation, fear and grief but with determination of purpose and cooperation between them, they overcome the problems of homelessness, hunger and fear that beset them. Ruth, Edek, Bronia and Jan are each very different characters, which provides opportunities to assess children's ability to explore different characters' motives and reactions to events on the journey. Ask the children questions as they read about how the characters are feeling at certain points. For example, ask: *When Jan is scornful about Edek's story of his frozen journey, how does that make Edek feel? When Edek follows Jan, what happens and how does Jan react?* Ask them to support their ideas with evidence from the text by asking: *Is there anything in the text that makes you think that?* Ruth, as the eldest, has the role of leader and is consistently honest, reliable and unselfish, but all the children display courage, loyalty, unselfishness and honesty at times. This provides an opportunity to assess children's abilities to understand dilemmas and the consequences of choices. For example, when Jan realises the silver sword is missing, ask them to suggest what Jan's best course of action should be. Encourage them to think of why Joe Wolski reacts as he does to Jan.

The author wrote the novel using a realistic style with detailed descriptions of the effects that war had on the landscape and the people. But he also included elements of humour. Ask the children to identify anything or any character that displays humour and ask why the author included it. How would the story be different if it was not lightened by some amusing moments?

Jan is the most complex character in the story. When the children do the assessment activity, their answers to the questions will demonstrate their abilities to empathise with Jan's character and to think beyond the obvious simple responses.

Why did Jan do that?

> **Objective:** To demonstrate an ability to read between the lines of a text and empathise with a character's feelings.
> **What you need:** Copies of *The Silver Sword*, photocopiable page 32, coloured pens.

What to do
● Remind the children of the work they have done during reading in investigating the characters' feelings and, in particular, the dilemmas that Jan faced.
● Provide the children with photocopiable page 32. Ask the children to work individually. Tell them to read the questions and write their answers in the spaces.
● Once they have answered the questions, ask them to read each one again and find the relevant section in the story.
● Invite them to check their answers against the story. They can add to or alter their original response, if they wish to improve it, using a different-coloured pen.
● Encourage them to make notes of key points on the reverse side of the photocopiable sheet as they check with the story to help them give their answers. Encourage them to write more than one sentence.
● Invite the children to give their answers orally, and then to choose the question where they think they have given the best final answer. Ask them to copy the question onto a sheet of paper and write their answers in full underneath.

Assessment

Why did Jan do that?

- Answer the questions below using your memory. For each question think about why he felt like that.
- Check your answers against the story. (You can use the back of this page to make notes, before writing your answers below.)
- Look over your answers again. Add anything that you think will improve your answers using a different-coloured pen.

Why did Jan smile when Ruth gave him his wooden box when he was found near the cellar?
Why was Jan scornful when Edek told his story on the train?
Why did Jan vanish when he learned about Bistro's escape from the zoo?
Why did Jan and Ludwig leave the others when they were only 80 miles from Switzerland?
Why did Jan burst into tears when he first saw the mountains?
Why did Jan abandon Ludwig to help his friends in the storm?

READ & RESPOND: Activities based on The Silver Sword